Orangeville Ontario Beginnings in Photos, Saving Our History One Photo at a Time

Photography
by Barbara Raué
2013

Series Name:
Cruising Ontario

Book 30: Orangeville Part 1

Cover photo: Orangeville Town Hall, 87 Broadway

Series Name: Cruising Ontario

Other Books by Barbara Raue

Coins of Gold

Arrows, Indians and Love

The Life and Times of Barbara
Volume 1: Inventions That Have Enhanced My Life
Volume 2: Entertainment That I Have Enjoyed
Volume 3: East Coast Trips
Volume 4: Olympics
Volume 5: Wonders of the World
Volume 6: Caribbean Cruises
Volume 7: Animals
Volume 8: Storms
Volume 9: Wars

The Cromwell Family Book

Orangeville

John Corbit acquired land in the area in 1829 and is one of the earliest settlers. Spring Brook, a tributary of the Credit River, provided water for power for several mills located downstream.

In 1833 Seneca Ketchum bought 200 acres on the north side of what became Broadway, followed four years later by George Grigg who bought 100 acres on the south side. By 1844 when Orange Lawrence and his wife, Sarah, arrived from Connecticut, a well-established community called Grigg's Mill existed beside Mill Creek. (Mill Creek and Spring Brook were the same tributary of the Credit River.)

Orange Lawrence helped to develop the community. He bought 300 acres, laid out the southeast part of town, bought Grigg's Mill, opened a general store and a tavern, built a second mill, founded the first school, and became the village's first postmaster in 1847. He left a strong mark on the community which took the appropriate name of Orangeville.

Immigrants from Ireland and other parts of the British Isles and Canada West came throughout the 1840s and 1850s with some establishing successful mixed farms while others settled in the village and became the landowners, merchants, and tradesmen whose needs lead to the development of good transportation routes.

By the 1860s it was increasingly difficult to deliver and receive goods to and from the supply centres in the south. Mono Road, Centre Road, Trafalgar Road, and the Toronto to Owen Sound Road were gravel roads that were difficult to traverse by horse and wagon for much of the year. Winter was the season when most goods were transported by sleigh over frozen roads.

By 1871 two daily stage lines were operating between Orangeville and Brampton, and that year the Toronto, Grey and Bruce Railway, a narrow gauge rail line, reached Orangeville, thanks to the efforts of town fathers such as Jesse Ketchum Jr., Samuel and Robert McKitrick, Johnston Lindsey, Thomas Jull, John Foley, and Dr. William Armstrong.

By 1875 there was a foundry, three planing mills, two saw mills, a tannery, a carding mill, several carriage and wagon manufacturers, and a successful pottery business in operation, along with four grocers, three hardware merchants, two drugstores, three watchmakers, three bakeries, and three establishments providing boots and shoes.

It was the foresight of Orange Lawrence and Jesse Ketchum that had large sections of land on either side of the main street laid out for both commercial and residential building lots. The south side followed Mill Creek while a regular grid pattern was determined for the streets on the north side from First to Fifth Streets both east and west and north to Fifth Avenue, with a wide main street called Broadway. This 30-metre (100-foot) avenue was not typical of Ontario towns of the time, but has proven to be very valuable over the years. In 1875 the Town Hall was constructed, and in 1887 the first telephone exchange was established, but it wasn't until 1916 that electricity came to the town.

The old town of Orangeville is still alive today. Some of the buildings on Broadway have been demolished; others have been renovated, while others remain as they were when they were built 120 years ago.

There are hundreds of old buildings in Orangeville which have retained their 1800s architectural styles and character. The first Orangeville book covers the beginnings of Orangeville with pictures from the south side of town, and buildings on Broadway. An appendix is included to describe architectural styles and terms which are referred to throughout the book. The second book covers buildings to the north of the town, as well as pictures taken in surrounding villages of Laurel, Caledon Village and Mono Centre.

Table of Contents

Beginnings of Orangeville – Bythia Street

22 Bythia Street – Vergeboard decoration – Gothic Revival

20 Bythia Street – Gothic Revival – dichromatic brickwork

16 Bythia Street – dichromatic brickwork

14 Bythia – Gothic

12 Bythia

10 Bythia – Mary Jane Bennett, Seamstress c. 1885

8 Bythia – John and Mary Ellen Haley, Merchant – c. 1891
Gothic Revival – decorative vergeboards on gables,
dichromatic brickwork, buff coloured voussoirs and lintels

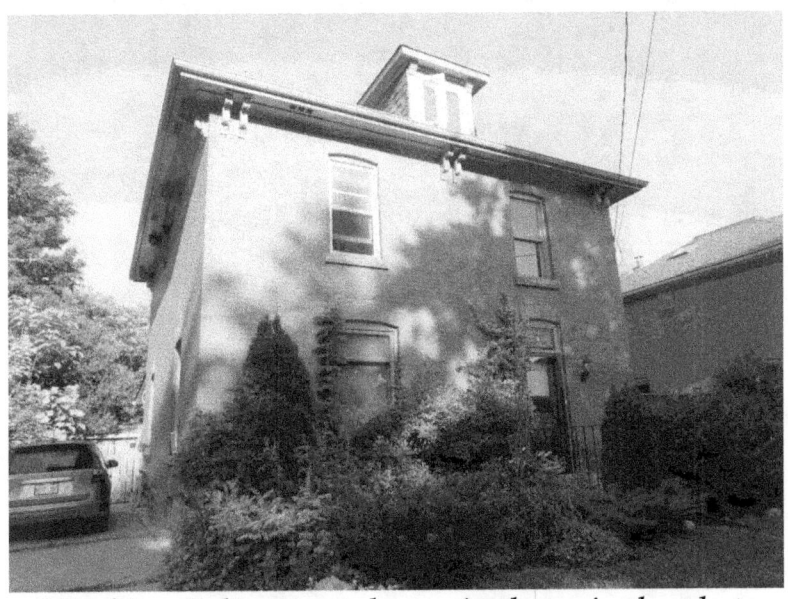

6 Bythia – Italianate style – paired cornice brackets

4 Bythia Street – Italianate – single cornice brackets

Dormer in the attic

28 York Street – Italianate with quoining on corners, paired cornice brackets, and Gothic Revival sharply pitched gable

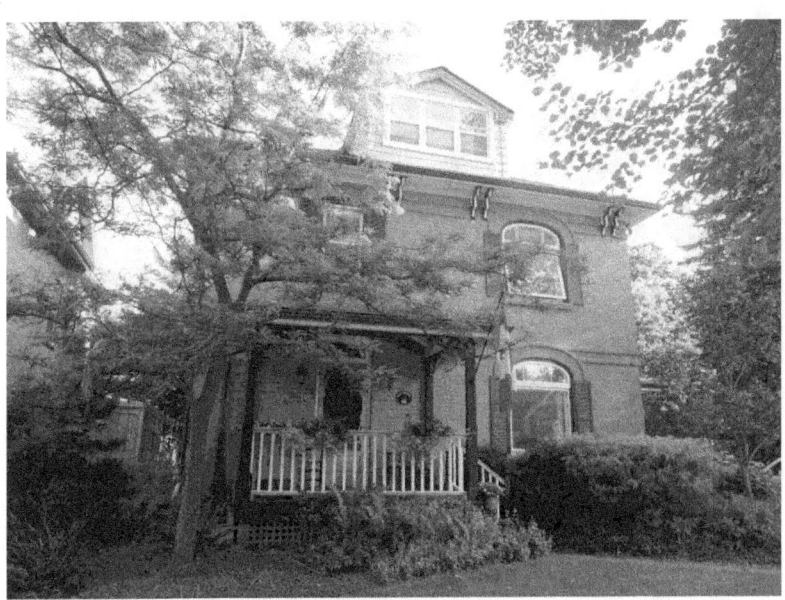

26 York Street – Italianate with paired cornice brackets

19 York Street – Gothic Revival with decorative Vergeboard on the sharply-pitched gable, bay window, buff-coloured voussoirs

Italianate style, paired cornice brackets, buff-coloured banding and voussoirs, bay window

17 York Street – Gothic Revival style with bay window – built by tanner George Campbell who operated the tannery on Little York Street – c. 1880

11 York Street – heavy stone lintels above and below the windows, and quoining on the corners, dormer in attic

16 York Street – Gothic Revival – Robert McKeown, shoemaker – c. 1877 – steeply-pitched gable roofs, dichromatic brickwork and flat-arched window openings

14 York Street – multi-coloured brick – newer building

12 York Street built by John Rowan – Italianate style with hipped roof, dichromatic brickwork, paired cornice brackets – wraparound porch is a more recent addition

10 York Street

7 York Street – Gothic Revival

6 York Street – Gothic Revial/Italianate – quoining on corners, paired cornice brackets, triangular pediment supported by columns

4 York Street – Italianate with triangular pediment with decorated tympanum, heavy stone voussoirs, paired cornice brackets

3 York Street – Vernacular Queen Anne– Primitive Methodist Chapel c. 1854 – turret added about 1911

2 York Street – built by W. Connell – McBride House c. 1902 - Romanesque style with massive shape, east-facing tower (ivy covered), large arches over front window and door opening, unusual keyhole-shaped window. When Tweedsmuir Presbyterian Church was built to the north of this property, the McBride House became the manse for the Presbyterian minister.

5 York Street – Gothic Revival

Little York Street

11 Little York Street – Italianate – buff-coloured brick banding
and keystones and voussoirs, paired cornice brackets

13-15 Little York Street – Gothic Revival style

17 Little York Street – Thomas Jull House, miller – c. 1858 –
Regency style with hip roof, large windows and bay windows
on the sides, originally clad in red brick and had a trellis
verandah (stuccoed later)

John Street

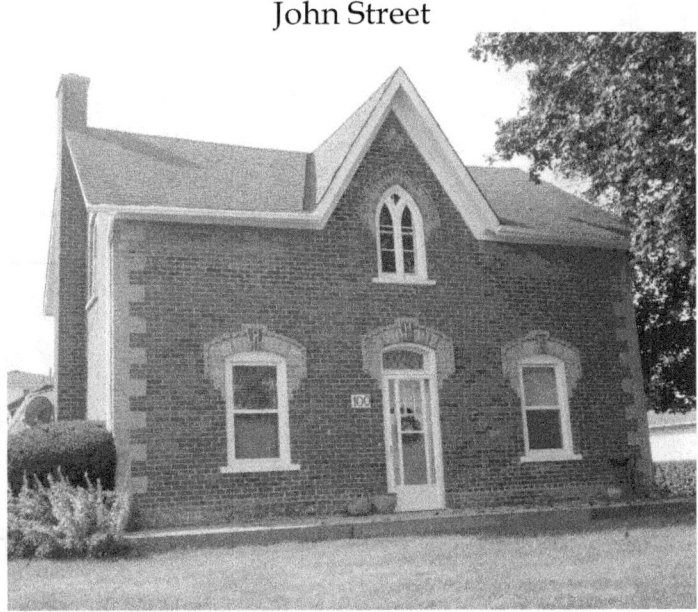

100 John Street – lancet window, buff-coloured voussoirs, dichromatic brickwork

24 John Street – Gothic Revival style – decorative vergeboard on sharpely pitched gable, bay window with paired cornice brackets

8 John Street –Lawrence House c. 1850 – built for Orange and Sarah Lawrence – Georgian style – 1½ storeys, large window openings, return eaves in the gable ends of the roof – underneath the siding is a stucco exterior over log

12 John Street- Italianate style

6 John Street – Tweedsmuir Memorial Presbyterian Church
1837, 1940 and 1959

Mill Street

51 Mill Street – Italianate style, paired cornice brackets, buff coloured banding, heavy stone voussoirs

53 Mill Street

56 Mill Street

58 Mill Street – Italianate, buff coloured banding, keystones
and voussoirs, dichromatic brickwork on corners, paired
cornice brackets – Joseph Foster, Contractor c. 1888

59 Mill Street

62 Mill Street – Italianate – wrap-around verandah, paired cornice brackets, dichromatic brickwork

63 Mill Street – Gothic Revival – decorative vergeboard

Italianate with second-storey door onto balcony

Iron cresting above bay window

68 Mill Street

71 Mill Street – John Richardson, Carpenter c. 1904

73 Mill Street

76 Mill Street – Joseph S. Hewitt, Carpenter c. 1870

80 Mill Street

86 Mill Street

91 Mill Street

88 Mill Street

87-89 Mill Street – John Bernard, Builder c. 1886

64 Mill Street

90 Mill Street – Ryan Hotel, Peavoy House c. 1873

105-107 Mill Street

109 Mill Street

22 Mill Street

Town Line Railway Station – the rail line connects the town with the CN main line in Brampton and the CP mainline in Streetsville

36 Wellington Street

30 Wellington Street – Christina and Frederick Marshall,
Saddler and Harness Maker c. 1877

28 Wellington Street

31 Wellington Street – iron crest work above bay window, decorative Vergeboard in steeply pitched gable

24 Wellington Street

25 Wellington Street

21 Wellington Street – Italianate style – arched voussoirs and keystones, wide eaves formerly with cornice brackets, dichromatic brickwork

20 Wellington Street

16-18 Wellington Street – King House c. 1888 - Second Empire
style – large brick house, mansard roof, ornamental ironwork

19 Wellington Street

7 Wellington Street – Gothic Revival
Edward and Adelaide Armstrong, Builder c. 1887

17 Wellington Street

10 Wellington Street – Andrew and Margaret Mara,
Shoemaker c. 1852

6 Wellington Street – buff-coloured keystones and voussoirs
Eliza and William Sutton, Stone Cutter c. 1876

4 Wellington Street

1 Wellington Street – Gothic Revival

2 Wellington Street – Armstrong Foundry c. 1896

Church Street

5 Church Street - Italianate

7 Church Street – Gothic Revival, two-tone brickwork

6 Church Street – Gothic Revival

8 Church Street – Gothic Revival – steeply pitched gable

9 Church Street – Robert and Carrie Allen, Blacksmith c. 1886

10 Church Street – Italianate – paired cornice brackets, dichromatic brickwork, quoining, balcony off door on 2nd storey

14 Church Street – Gothic Revival – arched voussoirs over windows and doorway

17 Church Street – Dods Kniting Mills c. 1913
Early Industrial Architecture

Armstrong Street

35 Armstrong Street – Canadian Pacific Railway Station – distinctive conical roof (witch's hat) covers former waiting room

Broadway Avenue

63 Broadway – James Graham – Tavern Keeper c 1852
Greystones Inn – Georgian style

65 Broadway
Edwardian Classicism – large triangular front gable with
Palladian window and shallow roofed porch

Gothic Revival style

78 Broadway – c. 1864
Gothic Revival with steeply pitched roof, decorative
bargeboard in the façade gable

113 Broadway

87 Broadway – Orangeville Town Hall – built to serve as town hall, municipal offices, market area, opera house – c. 1875 Italianate architecture with projecting roof eaves, paired cornice brackets, pedimented roof line, and use of contrasting brick colours – the cupola is a prominent feature

114 Broadway

117-123 Broadway – Italianate style with buff coloured brick, pointed windows with keystones of brown locally quarried sandstone, cornice with raised brick pattern using dentils and arches

123-127 Broadway

133 Broadway – dormer windows

148 Broadway – Jackson Block – Italianate – built between 1874 and 1875 (Thomas Jackson, saddler) – elaborate raised window hoods and lintels over the windows, red brick pilasters divide the façade into three bays, buff brick bracket at roofline, elaborate red and buff brick corbelled cornice tops the structure, pedimented roofline over the central bays

148 Broadway built between 1874 and 1875
Jackson Block – Italianate style with elaborate raised window
hoods, lintels over the windows, red brick pilasters divide the
block into three bays, red and buff brick corbelled cornice,
pedimented roofline

Mural of Grand Central Hotel

Mural of traffic on Broadway July 12, 1921

Mural

The decorative stonework on the Broadway and Mill Street facades is a hallmark of the Beaux-Arts Classicism style with the use of columns

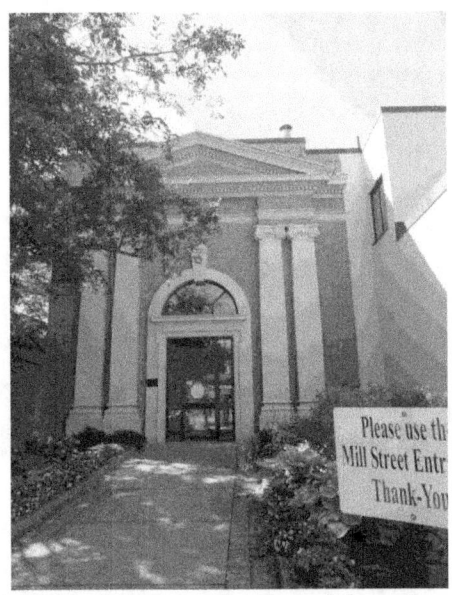

Orangeville Public Library recessed façade on Broadway

Orangeville Public Library 1907 – 1 Mill Street

153 Broadway c. 1876 – Italianate style – white limestone details enhancing the façade, dentil brick pattern across the roofline and repeated under the continuous limestone sills running under the windows on each storey

162 Broadway

166-168 Broadway

165-179 Broadway

177 Broadway

187-195 Broadway – Italianate – constructed for Mary Ketchum – upper floors with five-course buff brick banding, voussoirs are buff brick with a decorative raised edge, the pilasters are quoined in buff brick ending in a round topped brick design above the roof line.

205-207 Broadway – Italianate – decorative brickwork, second-storey door

Old Post Office – 216 Broadway – Chateau style
Two storey, built of limestone quarried in the Hockley Valley,
steeply pitched roof

Clock tower originally mounted on the
old Post Office building

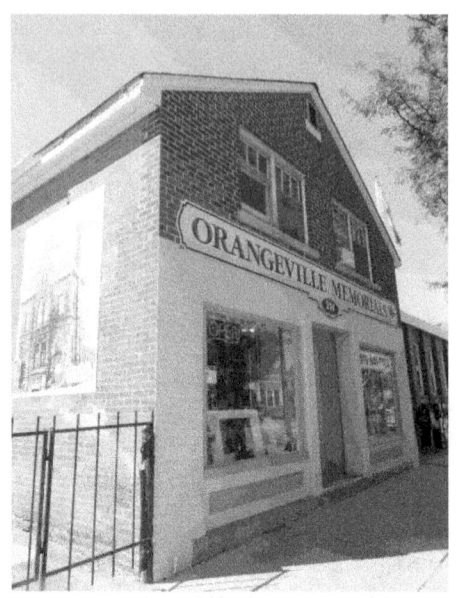

214 Broadway – Orangeville Memorials – Frontier style

237 Broadway – Italianate – dichromatic brickwork,
paired cornice brackets

Fire Hall built in A.D. 1891 in Italianate style with the original hose tower being 62 feet high and a 20,000-gallon reservoir located beneath the building. The fire bell sounded a 9 p.m. curfew for anyone under 16.

236 Broadway – two storey – Broadway Animal Hospital
Italianate style c. 1890s – home of Andrew Dods

238 Broadway – Regency Cottage – one-storey, low-pitched
hip roof, symmetrical front façade

239 Broadway – Aiken House built in 1896 in the
Queen Anne style – turret, gambrel roof, chimney with
vertical pilaster-like brick work detail

240 Broadway – Italianate – paired cornice brackets,
dichromatic brickwork, wrap-around veranda

248 Broadway – Italianate – single cornice brackets remain on porch, dormer in the attic

Broadway – Gothic Revival style, buff-coloured voussoirs, ornamental vergeboards hanging from the roof on the gable

243 Broadway – 1½ storey with dormers in the attic

245 Broadway – Italianate style – paired cornice brackets,
dichromatic brickwork

247 Broadway – Westminster United Church built in 1879 – originally Zion Presbyterian Church – Victorian Gothic Revival with a spire at the top finial to act as a lightning rod, lancet windows, steeply pitched roof lines, buttresses to strengthen the walls

250 Broadway – Italianate – quoining on the corners, paired cornice brackets

253 Broadway – dormer in attic

255 Broadway – Gothic Revival

257 Broadway – Italianate – wrap-around verandah, paired cornice brackets

Mural looking at Town Hall from south side of Broadway in 1930

260 Broadway – Irish Georgian style built in 1858 by Guy Leslie, an Irish immigrant – features a hip roof, central door and a balanced arrangement of windows with a pair of round top windows grouped together on the second floor. It became known as "Castle Leslie" by the locals.

269 Broadway – Italianate – wide porch

pediment (low gable over the door) with decorated
tympanum, decorative capitals on the pillars

267 Broadway – Italianate – paired cornice brackets, bay window

273 Broadway – Egan Funeral Home – Italianate style, paired cornice brackets, dichromatic brickwork, rounded window openings

283 Broadway – Romanesque – massive shape, tower on side and front, large arches over windows

283 Broadway – detail – decorative Vergeboard, paired cornice brackets

Tower, large arches over windows

283 Broadway from rear – a huge house

277 Broadway – Ellen McCabe and James Thompson, tailor
c. 1879 - Italianate

287 Broadway – Romanesque – tower, large arches over windows, paired cornice brackets, iron cresting

293 Broadway – Italianate – paired cornice brackets, buff coloured soldiering over windows, buff coloured quoining on corners

291 Broadway – Gothic Revival – pediment over doorway, bay window

Decorative vergeboard

295 Broadway – Gothic Revival – buff soldiering over windows, and buff brick quoining on corners

297 Broadway – Italianate – wide porch, stone lintels above and below windows

299 Broadway – Gothic Revival – sharply pitched gables, dichromatic brickwork, decorative cornice brackets, bay window, dormer in attic

301 Broadway – William and Jane Hall, retired farmer c. 1881 Gothic Revival – dichromatic brickwork

Architectural Terms

Belvedere: (from the Italian "beautiful view") an architectural feature on a roof, in a garden or on a terrace that gives a beautiful view. Example: 28 Zina Street	
Brackets: a decorative or weight-bearing structural element which forms a right angle with one side against a wall and the other under a projecting surface such as an eave or roof. Example: 34 Mill Street	
Buttress: a masonry structure built against or projecting from a wall which serves to support or reinforce the wall. In Canadian architecture, they are sometimes used for decoration. Example: 3 Zina Street	
Cornice: originally the wooden overhand of the roof. With the use of stone, brick, iron and steel, the cornice is any projecting shelf at the top of a ceiling or roof. They can be very decorative. Example: 117-123 Broadway	
Cupola: a small, dome-like structure on top of a building often used to provide a lookout or to admit light and air. Example: 87 Broadway (Town Hall)	
Dentil Moulding: an even series of rectangles used as ornamental decoration in cornices. Example: 187-192 Broadway	

Dichromatic brickwork: the use of two colours of brick, tile or slate to decorate a façade.	
Dormer: (French for "sleep") a gable end window that pierces through the plane of a sloping roof surface to create usable space in the top floor or attic of a building by adding headroom. Example: 135-139 Broadway	
Gable: the triangular portion of a wall between the edges of a sloping roof. Example: 16 York Street	
Gambrel Roof: a symmetrical two-sided roof with two slopes on each side; the upper slope is positioned at a shallow angle, while the lower slope is steep. It is similar to a mansard roof, but a gambrel has vertical gable ends instead of being hipped at the four corners of the building. Example: 239 Broadway	
Hipped Roof: a roof where all sides slope downwards to the walls with no gables. Example: 34 Mill Street	
Keystones and Voussoirs: a voussoir is a wedge-shaped element used in building an arch. A keystone is the central stone that locks all the stones into position, allowing the arch to bear weight. A keystone is often enlarged and embellished. Example: 117-123 Broadway	

Lancet Window: a tall, narrow window with a pointed arch at its top. Example: 3 Zina Street	
Mansard Roof: This style was popularized by Francois Mansart (1598-1666), an accomplished architect of the French Baroque period and especially fashionable during the Second French Empire (1852-1870). This roof is almost flat on the top section, with two slopes on each of its sides with the lower slope at a steeper angle than the upper and having dormer windows. Example: 16/18 Wellington Street	
Palladian Window: a large window that is divided into three sections with the centre section larger than the two side sections and usually arched. Example: 24 Zina Street	
Pediment: a triangular section above the horizontal structure (entablature), typically supported by columns. The inside of the triangle is called the tympanum. Example: 51 Zina Street	
Pilaster: a slightly projecting column built into or applied to the face of a wall for additional structural support. Example: 148 Broadway	
Quoin: masonry blocks at the corner of a wall, often a decorative feature, usually larger or of a different colour than the rest of the wall. Example: 6 York Street	

Rose Window: a circular window with ornamental tracery radiating from the centre. Example: 3 Zina Street	
Sidelight: a window, usually with a vertical emphasis, that flanks a door, and is often used to emphasize the importance of a primary entrance. Example: 14 Second Street, or 238 Broadway	
Vergeboards: also called bargeboards – hang from the projecting end of a roof and are often elaborately carved and ornamented. Example: 16 York Street	

Orangeville's Building Styles

Georgian, before 1860 – This style began with the British King Georges in the 18th century. These buildings have balanced facades around a central door, medium-pitched gable roofs, and small paned windows. Example: 260 Broadway	
Regency Cottage, 1830-1860 – This style originated in England in 1815 and spread to Ontario later in the 19th century as British officers retired to Canada. It is a modest one-storey house with a low-pitched hip roof and has a symmetrical front façade. Example: 11 First Street	
Gothic Revival, 1830-1890 – These decorative buildings have sharply-pitched gables with highly detailed vergeboards, pointed-arch window openings, and dichromatic brickwork. It is a common style in Ontario. Examples: 20 Wellington Street, 67 Zina Street	
Italianate, 1850-1900 – It has wide-bracketed eaves, belvederes, wrap-around verandahs. Examples: 12 York Street, 62 Zina Street	
Second Empire, 1860-1880 – The mansard roof is the most noteworthy feature of this style and is evidence of the French origins. Projecting central towers and one or two-storey bays can also be present. Example: 16-18 Wellington Street	
Romanesque Revival, 1880-1910 – This style hearkens back to medieval architecture of the 11th and 12th centuries with a heavy appearance, blocky towers and rounded arches. Example: 2 York Street	

Queen Anne, 1885-1900 – This style is distinguished by an irregular outline featuring a combination of an offset tower, broad gables, projecting two-storey bays, verandahs, multi-sloped roofs, and tall, decorative chimneys. A mixture of brick and wood is common. Windows often have one large single-paned bottom sash and small panes in the upper sash. Example: 239 Broadway	
Edwardian, 1900-1930 – This style bridges the ornate and elaborate styles of the Victorian era and the simplified styles of the 20th century. Balanced facades, simple roof lines, dormer windows, large front porches, and smooth brick surfaces are its characteristics. Example: 24 Zina Street	
Art Moderne, 1930-1945 – This style originated in the United States with rounded corners, smooth walls, and flat roofs. Large expanses of glass were used, even wrapping around corners. Example: former Orangeville Dairy, 5 First Street	

www.ingramcontent.com/pod-product-compliance
Lightning Source LLC
Chambersburg PA
CBHW051343170526
45166CB00002B/929